Unchained

Democratising Business Through Blockchain Technology

Table of Contents

Chapter 1. Introduction

In the Special Report, 'Unchained: Democratizing Business Through Blockchain Technology,' we unravel the complexities of a rapidly evolving digital landscape and illustrate how blockchain technology is reshaping the traditional business operations. Move beyond the buzzwords and dive into a comprehensive exploration of this transformative technology, stripped of unnecessary jargon and served in an approachable format. Whether you're a novice in the technical world or an experienced business leader, this report will elevate your understanding of blockchain's potential and how it is already disrupting various industries. Be inspired by the possibilities and let this report prepare you for the decentralized future that lies ahead. This is your chance to be ahead of the curve, equipped with knowledge that could redefine your business, all in the turn of the pages of this Special Report.

Chapter 2. Setting the Digital Stage: Understanding Blockchain

Blockchain technology is considered one of the most transformative innovations in modern times, and justifiably so, as it barrels its way through traditional business operations, reshaping the way we perceive trust, transparency, and value exchange. Understanding what lies beneath the surface of this disruptive technology is key in envisaging how we can leverage its immense potential.

2.1. Blockchain: A Brief Introduction

Often characterized as a disruptive force, Blockchain is the underlying technology powering cryptocurrencies like Bitcoin. However, its applications extend beyond just cryptocurrencies, finding its way into every facet of business and governance due to its ability to create a decentralized, secure, transparent and efficient system for data recording and transactions.

This technology, at its core, is a chain of digital "blocks" that contain records of transactions. Each block is connected to all the blocks before and after it, creating an immutable and near-indestructible record of data or transaction history.

2.2. The Fundamentals of Blockchain

The fundamental elements of Blockchain technology make it uniquely suited for application across several sectors. These elements include:

Decentralization: In a traditional centralized system such as a bank, all data is stored in a single centralized database. This brings inherent risks such as data hacking and an over-reliance on a single entity. Blockchain technology invalidates these concerns as it stores data across a network of computers, decentralizing its storage and ensuring no single entity has absolute power over the network.

Immutability: This simply means that once data is stored in a block, it is extremely difficult to change or erase. This is because each block is secured and bound to each other using cryptographic principles. This feature enhances the reliability and accuracy of data stored on a blockchain.

Transparency: Another quintessential feature of blockchain is transparency. While user identity is secure and anonymized, all transactions are made public on the ledger. This makes it a fantastic tool for creating transparent operations in any business or field of work.

Security: The use of cryptographic techniques in creating and linking blocks on a blockchain ensures that hacking into the system is a near impossible task. This inherent high-security quotient makes blockchain an attractive choice for sensitive information and transaction records.

2.3. The Reinvention of Trust in Digital Age

In today's digital age, the definition of trust is undergoing a significant transformation. Instead of traditional intermediaries like banks or governments, users are quickly transitioning to place their trust in cryptographic algorithms and the underlying principles of decentralization and transparency in a blockchain network.

The unique structure and mechanisms of blockchain provide

assurance that data and transactions are secure, traceable, and immutable. This creates a robust, tamper-proof system that allows parties to interact and transact with confidence without the need for intermediaries.

2.4. Real-World Applications of Blockchain

Blockchain's potential isn't abstract; it's being realized in many industries worldwide. Blockchain-based applications are beginning to emerge, spanning various sectors such as supply chain management, healthcare, finance, and public administration, among others.

In supply chain management, for example, blockchain can enhance transparency and traceability, enabling real-time tracking of products from the producer to the consumer. In healthcare, blockchain technology can help secure and streamline patient records while ensuring confidentiality and compliance. Similarly, in finance, blockchain can revolutionize traditional banking systems, allowing for faster, secure, and cost-effective transactions.

2.5. The Challenges Ahead

Despite its numerous advantages, there are also challenges that need to be addressed before blockchain can be fully actualized. These include the technology's high energy consumption, the current lack of regulatory framework, and issues concerned with scalability. However, with continued research and investment, it's expected that these challenges will eventually be mitigated.

2.6. Looking to the Future

Blockchain presents endless possibilities, each with the potential to redefine how we engage in digital transactions and data management. As we continue to develop and refine this technology, the extent of its impact on our lives promises to be profound.

Indeed, breaking away from traditional norms of business operations and opening up to radical new systems like blockchain might seem like a daunting task, but the rewards could be substantial. By setting the stage for the decentralization of trust and the democratization of secure and transparent transactions, blockchain is paving the way for a truly global digital economy. Whether you are a novice seeking fundamental understanding or a seasoned business leader looking for ways to innovate, the journey towards a blockchain-enabled future is worth embarking on.

Chapter 3. The Genesis of Blockchain: An Explorative History

The emergence of blockchain technology sparked a revolutionary shift in various sectors, from finance to supply chain management, healthcare, and beyond. Its decentralized, secure, and transparent nature is heralded as the ultimate solution to many traditional business challenges.

Chapter 4. Early Models and Preconditions

The foundational principles for blockchain technology have their roots in computer science and cryptography. For decades, researchers have been grappling with problems like secure communication, time-stamping digital documents, and digital currency. It was the culmination of these complex problems, that set the stage for the development of blockchains.

In 1982, a computer scientist named David Chaum proposed a digital money system concept in his paper, "Blind Signatures for Untraceable Payments." He introduced cryptographic protocols that could uphold privacy without any reliance on trust. Since then, this concept was further developed and refined into what is today known as the 'digital cash' concept.

Chapter 5. First Functioning Blockchains

Interestingly, the term "blockchain" was not coined until the launch of Bitcoin in 2009. It was a system that a pseudonymous person (or group) by the name of Satoshi Nakamoto presented. Nakamoto introduced blockchain as a public ledger containing all transaction data from anyone who uses bitcoin. Transactions are entered chronologically in a blockchain which is how cryptocurrencies keep track of digital currency transactions.

Nakamoto's creation of Bitcoin paved the way for more advanced use of blockchain technology beyond cryptocurrency. He solved two key challenges to digital cash: preventing double-spending without a central authority and creating consensus within a decentralized network.

Chapter 6. Introducing Smart Contracts

In 2013, a new development of blockchain gave birth to a wider application: the introduction of smart contracts by Ethereum. Smart contracts are programmable scripts that trigger actions when certain conditions are met. They offered a new layer of functionality, taking blockchain beyond financial transactions and into a broad array of potential applications. For instance, verifying the validity of a claim, automating governance, voting systems, and many more.

Chapter 7. Advancements in Decentralized Platforms

The blockchain community did not stop at smart contracts. In 2014, Dan Larimer proposed the next evolution: Delegated Proof-of-Stake (DPoS) blockchains. These are faster and more efficient blockchains where coin holders vote on 'delegates' to confirm transactions and maintain the blockchain.

In 2017, the development of InterPlanetary File System (IPFS) and Filecoin allowed blockchains to store data across a distributed network of nodes. This technology now supports the decentralized web, where websites and applications run without a central server.

Chapter 8. Mutual Distributed Ledger (MDL)

The Mutual Distributed Ledger (MDL, also known as multi-organizational blockchain) came into the scene around 2015. Instead of one central database storing all transactions and balances, multiple copies of the same database exist across various participants. The radical innovation of MDL is that control and security are decentralized, providing a single digital version of the truth that participants can trust even without trusting each other.

Chapter 9. Blockchain Today

Today, we see numerous public and private blockchain initiatives reshaping industries. From decentralized finance (DeFi) protocols to supply chain tracking, blockchain is impacting sectors beyond just finance. Other case studies include intellectual property protection, reducing the cost of transaction and verification, enhancing transparency and traceability, amongst others.

The future of blockchain is still evolving, with ongoing research to address challenges such as scalability, privacy, and energy consumption. Regardless, the potential of blockchain technology is undeniable. Its implications have already begun to disrupt traditional operations, sparking a paradigm shift in the business world.

In conclusion, blockchain technology has traveled a long way since its inception. The aura of intrigue and potential around it continues to grow. Considering the relatively short timeline of its existence, the blockchain's impact on the global landscape is remarkable. As we move forward, it would be wise to trace its trajectory and prepare for the waves of change it promises. It is only by understanding its past that we are able to invest wisely in its future. This continues to be the best approach when dealing with paradigm-shifting technologies like the blockchain.

Chapter 10. The Nuts and Bolts: How Blockchain Works

To provide a robust understanding of blockchain technology, it's important to start at the basic level, defined by its operational components and mechanisms. This aids in building a strong foundation and accurately comprehending how blockchain works.

10.1. Understanding The Foundation

Blockchain is essentially a distributed ledger system. Like a traditional ledger that records financial transactions, a blockchain stores and verifies data across multiple computers spread globally. Each piece of data, or 'block,' is linked to the others in a chronological 'chain', ensuring the integrity and permanence of the data stored within.

Let's comprehend each component:

1. **Block:** A block is a package for data storage, unique because it contains a 'hash,' or unique code, that distinguishes it from every other block. Notably, each block also houses the hash of the previous block, creating an unbroken chain of data.

2. **Chain:** The chain links the blocks together. Each subsequent block contains the unique hash of the preceding block, thereby forming the chain. Any change in one block's data alters its hash. Since this block's hash is stored in the next block, a cascade effect occurs – changing the data in one block invalidates the entire chain. This feature mitigates the risk of modification or fraud.

3. **Node:** Every computer connected to the blockchain network, or 'node,' receives a full copy of the blockchain. This decentralization furthers security since any attempted change must occur across a majority of the nodes, a near-impossible task

given the scale of networks.

Let us now venture deeper into the mechanisms at play.

10.2. Proof of Work

Blockchain technologies often use 'Proof of Work' (PoW). PoW is a consensus algorithm where 'miners' solve complex mathematical problems to append a block to the blockchain; this consumes computational power and time, hence the term 'work.'

PoW algorithm ensures security, as altering historic data would require redoing the work. Given the time and computational power needed, this makes fraudulent modifications unlikely.

10.3. Distributed Ledger and Decentralization

The distributed ledger technology (DLT) and decentralization are keystones of blockchain's architecture. The DLT serves as the core database, replicated and synchronized across the network. Rather than a central authority controlling the database, DLT provides each network user a copy of the complete historical and transactional data.

Decentralization eradicates the need for intermediaries and engenders trust and transparency. Blockchain's decentralized nature allows the entire network to validate transactions, maintaining data integrity and veracity.

10.4. Blockchain's Immutable Character

Immutability refers to the unalterable nature of the blockchain's historic records. Once a transaction is verified and added to the blockchain, altering it is next to impossible due to the hash function described earlier.

Immutability confers attractiveness to industries plagued by fraud, plagiarism, and tampering, as it guarantees integrity and safety of the stored data.

10.5. Smart Contracts and Automation

A smart contract is a piece of code stored in a blockchain that automatically executes when predefined conditions are met. By removing the need for intermediaries, smart contracts ensure transparency, expedite transactions, and reduce cost.

In terms of business operations, smart contracts enable automated consensus and transacting, thus streamlining the business processes while maintaining a secure and transparent environment.

10.6. Public vs Private Blockchains

There are two primary types of blockchains: Public and Private. A public blockchain network is open to anyone to participate, whereas a private blockchain restricts access, typically to a specific industry or organization.

Public blockchains are truly decentralized. However, they may suffer from scalability issues. Private blockchains, though centralized to an extent, resolve the scalability problem at the cost of some decentralization.

This understanding of blockchain technology, its mechanisms, and its features provides a strong foundation upon which to explore blockchain's vast potential and its application across various industries. The revolution is not simply about the technology itself, but how its concepts of decentralization, distributed power, and verified trustworthiness can incite fundamental changes in existing systems. And thus, demystify the complexities surrounding this transformative technology.

Chapter 11. Decentralization: The Elemental Change

Decentralization is not a new concept. We've seen it in multiple forms throughout history, from the Athenian idea of democracy to freedom of the press. At its core, decentralization is about dispersing power from a centralized authority. It's about promoting autonomy and creating systems where every participant has an influence. Enter blockchain technology.

11.1. The Fundamental Shift

Until recently, most businesses and institutions have operated in a centralized manner. Data and decision-making power are primarily located at the top level, rendering lower tiers subservient to the executive trustees. This top-down approach may have ensured control and consistency, but it has also led to several challenges such as inefficiencies, lack of innovation, and vulnerability to failures and attacks.

Blockchain proposes a departure from the traditional top-down hierarchical model, helping us embrace a more egalitarian form of functioning. Instead of a single, central authority, decision-making power and data control are distributed across the blockchain network. This horizontal distribution of power is the fundamental shift that comes with blockchain-enabled decentralization.

11.2. Rooted in Trust

Centralization primarily breeds mistrust as it inherently creates a divide between those with access and those without. Blockchain technology, with its innate transparency and security, builds the foundation for trust in a decentralized environment. While in a conventional structure, this trustworthiness would require a central control unit, blockchain generates it through cryptography and consensus protocols. It essentially makes every node in its network a point of validation, thereby creating a synergy of trust that is bigger than any single entity.

11.3. Blockchain and Peer-to-Peer Networks

The architecture of blockchain technology is a natural fit for Peer-to-Peer (P2P) networks. Traditionally, for transferring information or performing transactions in the digital space, we have depended on intermediaries or centralized entities who would authorize, validate and log the transactions. With blockchain, the need for such intermediaries could potentially disappear.

In a P2P network supported by blockchain, transactions can occur directly between parties without the need for a middleman. This accelerates the transaction speed, de-bureaucratizes the process, and reduces dependency, whilst enhancing security and privacy.

11.4. Bridging Geographies and Industries

Blockchain has the potential to move beyond the digital realm to adapt to physical realities and bridge across industries and over borders. By leveraging blockchain's decentralized feature, businesses can break geographical barriers, thereby opening doors to international collaborations and building global partnerships with ease. In this way, blockchain decentralization lays the groundwork for a global village in its truest form.

11.5. Challenges Along The Path

While the transformative potential of blockchain-based decentralizational is alluring, it doesn't come without stringent trials. Matters concerning security, regulatory frameworks, data privacy, and acceptance within societal norms are some of the key points of concern for blockchain's march towards a decentralized future.

11.6. Potential Realms of Disruption

Practically every industry stands to gain something from blockchain's decentralization. Healthcare, finance, supply chain, governance, and academia – the possibilities are endless. The pertinent questions like 'How?' and 'When?' still loom large, but what is certain is that a decentralized way of functioning, propelled by blockchain technology, is no longer a distant dream.

Creatives may find an avenue for fair value for their work through tokenized assets. Healthcare professionals might access a single source of verifiable, immutable patient data improving the standard of care. Financers could possibly see a financial world unbound by locational restrictions or middlemen. The possibilities, like the technology, are revolutionary.

As we step towards this new era of decentralized business frameworks, it is essential to venture forth with a comprehensive understanding of its underlying principles and the formidable changes it can bring. The blockchain revolution, much like earlier ones, will carry its unique benefits and challenges, which our society must be prepared to navigate. In this process, we will undoubtedly unlearn, relearn, and reshape our existing practices. Thus, the journey toward decentralization, crystallized through the lens of blockchain technology, is not just a technical one, but a truly transformative one.

Chapter 12. Dismantling Barriers: Blockchain's Role in Democratizing Business

The evolution of digital technology has been nothing short of incredible, marking significant advances in virtually every field. However, certain roadblocks continue impeding businesses and their operations. Blockchain technology holds the potential to dismantle these barriers, offering increased transparency, unassailable security, lower costs, and indefinite accessibility. Consequently, blockchain is transcending traditional norms of business operations, offering lucrative opportunities for both conventional and modern businesses.

12.1. The Impregnable Fortress of Security

Security continues to be a significant concern for businesses, especially with the emerging technological landscape. Blockchain technology does not merely increase the level of security operations; it revolutionizes it. Instead of centralized databases, susceptible to breaches and unauthorized access, blockchain's distributed ledger technology (DLT) provides an impregnable fortress of security.

In a blockchain network, each transaction is recorded and distributed across different nodes or computers on the network. Consequently, altering a single transaction record requires modifying all the related records on the entire network, a feat that is virtually impossible to achieve due to the consensus protocol in place.

12.2. The Manual of Transparency and Trust

Transparency and trust are the cornerstones of any business relationship. Yet, in a world of rapid digitalization, creating lasting trust-based associations faces numerous challenges. Blockchain technology, with its ability to maintain records that can be traced, reviewed, and audited by authorized parties, serves as a manual of transparency and trust.

The immutable and traceable nature of blockchain transactions provides a single source of truth, reducing the scope for disputes and fraudulent transactions. While the data is secured and only accessible by authorized parties, all transactions are transparently available within this closed group, fostering trust.

12.3. The Advantages Gate

To appreciate blockchain's potential in dismantling barriers, it's crucial to evaluate its cost-effectiveness. Blockchain reduces transaction costs by eliminating intermediaries, facilitating peer-to-peer transactions. From banking to supply chains, sectors that traditionally relied on brokers or intermediaries stand to benefit substantially from this innovation.

Consider international remittances, traditionally an expensive affair due to exchange rates and service charges. Blockchain provides a cheaper, faster alternative, a clear demonstration of its potential to democratize business.

Further, blockchain systems can be programmed to execute contracts - dubbed 'smart contracts'. These contracts automatically enforce obligations and terms without manual intervention, thereby reducing operational costs and potential human error.

12.4. The Road of Uninterrupted Accessibility

Envisage a future where time zones, geographic location, or operational hours do not limit businesses. Blockchain opens the door to this future with its potential for 24/7 accessibility and borderless operations.

As a public ledger on a peer-to-peer network, blockchain systems are continuously available for transactions, unfettered by time zones or geography. This unlimited access opens the international market for businesses of all sizes, effectively democratizing global business participation.

12.5. The Canvas of Innovation and Disruption

Blockchain technology is not restricted to financial transactions or contractual obligations. Its ability to authenticate data across various nodes in the network introduces a broad spectrum of applications for several sectors.

For instance, in the healthcare sector, blockchain can maintain incorruptible patient records and guarantee their security. Similarly, in the supply chain, blockchain can track goods from production to delivery, ensuring transparency and reducing counterfeit incidents.

Blockchain's ability to facilitate decentralized applications (DApps) further expands its potential. By supporting the development of decentralized social media platforms, voting systems, or cloud storage, blockchain technology heralds ground-breaking innovations, breaking existing operational norms.

12.6. Conclusion: The Path to Democratization

The power of blockchain to revolutionize business lies in its decentralized design, unassailable security, and unparalleled transparency. As pioneers explore its potential, the narrative around blockchain continues to shift from its association with cryptocurrencies to its ability to dismantle operational barriers.

Undeniably, embracing blockchain comes with challenges namely, regulatory issues, the need for extensive knowledge, and overcoming resistance to adoption. However, the transformative potential of this technology outweighs the obstacles. As we continue to embrace the digital frontier, blockchain technology holds promising prospects for businesses, large and small, heralding a more inclusive and democratic industry, ready to engage with the world in ways previously unimaginable.

Chapter 13. Industries in Upheaval: Case Studies of Blockchain Impact

Blockchain technology, often hailed as the most significant technological innovation since the internet, is drastically changing various industries. It brings about a new level of transparency, efficiency, and security that was previously unimaginable. The following sections detail how blockchain technology is creating a significant upheaval in various industries through a collection of comprehensive case studies.

13.1. The Financial Services Industry

The financial services industry offers the most lucid examples of blockchain's transformative impact. Traditional banking and financial systems are known for their inefficiency, characterized by lengthy processing times and lack of transparency. Blockchain has presented a solution to these challenges.

For instance, Ripple, a FinTech company, utilizes a decentralized ledger, RippleNet, to facilitate faster and cheaper international transactions. Before Ripple, international transactions often took several days and incurring hefty fees. RippleNet provides a frictionless transfer of funds across borders in just a few seconds.

Notably, the traditional financial system's inefficiencies led to the invention of Bitcoin, the first application of blockchain technology. Bitcoin introduced a decentralized alternative to traditional currency, governed by mathematical algorithms instead of a central authority, prompting many to reassess the value proposition of conventional financial institutions.

13.2. The Healthcare Industry

Blockchain's utility extends far beyond finance. In the healthcare sector, blockchain technology is helping address problems related to privacy and integrity of health records, supply chain management, and clinical trials.

For instance, Blockchain Health Company is leveraging distributed ledger technology to improve patient consent management and data sharing in clinical trials. Physician inefficiencies in obtaining patient consent and sharing data can delay these trials by months, and in some cases, years. Utilizing blockchain technology, complex administrative functions are streamlined, saving time, and improving patient privacy.

In another use case, pharmaceutical company MediLedger uses blockchain to enhance the integrity of drug supply chains. This application helps track pharmaceuticals from production to patient, combating counterfeit medication and improving patient safety.

13.3. The Supply Chain Industry

Supply chain management is another industry where blockchain technology is causing disruption. VeChain, a blockchain platform, is increasing transparency and trust in supply chains.

In traditional supply chain management, tracking a product's lifecycle is a laborious process prone to errors and manipulation. VeChain makes this process more transparent, allowing consumers, retailers, and manufacturers to track products from origin to end consumer.

By doing so, VeChain helps businesses prove their products'

authenticity, thereby increasing consumer confidence. For consumers, this means access to information that supports informed buying decisions, like being sure that a product claiming to be fair trade has indeed followed an ethical supply chain.

13.4. The Energy Industry

Blockchain also holds potential in the energy sector. Traditional energy markets are monopolized by a few large companies, making it difficult for smaller producers to enter. Blockchain can democratize the energy industry by making it possible for small-scale producers to participate.

For instance, LO3 Energy has created a peer-to-peer energy trading platform using blockchain. This platform enables small-scale producers, like home solar panel owners, to sell excess energy directly to their neighbors. The blockchain in this case serves as a tamper-proof record of energy production and consumption, ensuring fair trade.

To sum it up, these case studies prove that blockchain technology is on course to revolutionize not just the financial world but a broad array of sectors. It's ushering us into a new era of efficiency, transparency, and democracy in business operations. Its capabilities make it much more than a disruptive technology. It's potentially a foundational technology that could reshape the world as we know it.

With blockchain technology, industries are indeed in an upheaval. The way forward is to embrace this change, understand the implications of a decentralized environment and gear up for a blockchain-powered future.

Chapter 14. Future Predictions: The Expansive Potential of Blockchain

Blockchain technology, in its nascent yet rapidly evolving state, holds an unlimited potential for transforming major economic, political, and social structures. As with any novel technology, futurecasting its implications and influences is not an exact science. Yet, it is essential to explore possible trajectories to prepare and plan for impending shifts and disruptions.

14.1. The Democratization of Financial Services

The traditional financial system has always been influenced by a few dominant intermediaries, from big banks to insurance companies. With blockchain technology, the power can be transferred into the hands of the people. Decentralized finance, or DeFi, is a burgeoning field that leverages blockchain for peer-to-peer financial services. From lending and borrowing to investment and insurance, smart contracts can automate financial interactions that traditionally needed intermediaries.

This can fundamentally shift how we think about finance and economy. On one hand, DeFi can democratize access to financial services, especially for the unbanked and underbanked population. On the other, it can significantly reduce costs by taking out profit-seeking middlemen while providing faster and more efficient services.

14.2. A Trustless Economy

Blockchain's fundamental feature is its ability to establish trust. A trustless economy would mean an ecosystem where transactions and interactions are guaranteed not by traditional arbitrators or intermediaries but by transparent, verifiable, and immutable code. This is not limited to economic transactions but can pervade all aspects of society where trust is a necessary component.

Supply chains and product authenticity are some early benefactors of this trustless economy. Through blockchain's immutable records, businesses can offer consumers transparency and verifiability about product sources and thereby instill confidence. In industries rife with counterfeit products, such as pharmaceuticals, luxury goods, and food, blockchain can create a more reliable and secure scenario.

14.3. Government Systems and Voting

Governments and electoral systems worldwide can significantly benefit from blockchain technology. With the ability to provide transparency, immutability, and security, blockchain could reimagine voting and decision-making structures. Digital identities secured on a blockchain can ensure one-person-one-vote, eliminate voter fraud, and even ensure the anonymity of votes.

Governments could conduct procurements, allocate resources, and make decisions based on public consensus through more democratic and transparent processes. This could fundamentally change the public's relationship with the government, foster more active citizen engagement, and create an environment that breeds innovation and progress.

14.4. The Internet of Things (IoT)

Coupling blockchain technology with IoT devices constructs a future where everyday items, from refrigerators to cars, can interact securely and autonomously on our behalf. Smart contracts on a blockchain will enable devices to make decisions based on preset conditions. For example, a refrigerator with the ability to track its content could order groceries when it detects a shortage.

This has profound implications for industries like supply chain, manufacturing, and healthcare, where device interactions can be automated and connected into one reliable system. This ability to ensure device interactions without a centralized authority can increase efficiency, reduce costs, and allow for greater innovation.

14.5. Privacy and Freedom Online

In an era where data breaches and misuse are rife, blockchain provides a way to reclaim data ownership. Cryptography secures personal data on the blockchain, and thanks to the transparent nature of the technology, people can decide who gets to access their data and deny permission when necessary.

By decentralizing the internet - dWeb or Web 3.0 - blockchain stands the chance to redefine our relationship with the digital world. It could fuel a new era of decentralized platforms, where creators can publish their work without a middleman and interact directly with their audience.

As we hover on the precipice of the fourth industrial revolution, blockchain technology could be force pushing us towards a more equitable and prosperous future. Its potential applications are extensive and astounding, reminding us to remain open to the novel ways it could shape our world. However, the road to achieving these projections is fraught with potential setbacks and challenges, including technological limitations, regulatory issues, and adoption hurdles. These issues necessitate address, for us to ensure that the immense potential of blockchain is harnessed and directed constructively. But for now, this decentralized technology brings with it a promise to shift the power dynamics and build an infrastructural base for a more transparent, trustless, and inclusive world.

Chapter 15. Overcoming Challenges: The Constraints & Critics of Blockchain

The application and implementation of blockchain technology is not without challenges. Multiple constraints complicate the smooth functioning of the system, some of which are inherent to the technology, others a consequence of the nascent stage of blockchain's evolution or socio-economic factors. This chapter will discuss these constraints along with the criticisms that question its widespread deployment.

15.1. Understanding the Technological Hurdles

Benchmarking against traditional technologies, blockchain systems demonstrate a considerable gap in terms of performance and efficiency. The most frequently cited blockchain, Bitcoin, can only handle seven transactions per second while credit card provider Visa handles approximately 1,700 transactions per second. There is a significant performance discrepancy.

To preserve decentralization and security, blockchain relies on a consensus mechanism that verifies and validates transactions. With the most commonly used mechanism, proof-of-work, this process is intentionally slow and requires significant computational power, leading to scalability issues. Given, the quadratic scaling nature of blockchain, more transactions mean larger blocks, which in turn increase the time required for block propagation and validation, further emphasizing the scalability problem.

Scalability is particularly significant for public blockchains that aspire to process a high volume of transactions and house many apps. Some solutions propose "sharding" or compartmentalizing the network. However, the technology is still at the development stage and determining best practices is challenging.

15.2. Navigating Regulation and Legal Uncertainties

Legal and regulatory challenges also weigh heavy on blockchain. Because it's a cross-jurisdictional technology, policies differ significantly across national borders. Factors such as data privacy, consumer protection, tax policy, securities regulation, and investigations into fraudulent or illegal transactions are important considerations. Some countries are welcoming, but others ban cryptocurrencies entirely due to risks and instability.

Lawmakers and regulators worldwide are grappling with how to adapt existing legislation and invent new laws to accommodate, or even encourage, blockchain development. The goal is to enforce the law without stifling innovation; however, the challenge is substantial. The very nature of blockchain's decentralization resists traditional methods of control, the rules must be written into the protocol itself.

15.3. Energy Consumption and Environmental Impact

High energy usage is another significant concern for blockchain. With Bitcoin blockchain, the consensus protocol uses proof of work which requires miners to solve complex mathematical problems, resulting in substantial energy usage. The extent of the problem is so significant that Bitcoin's energy usage rivals that of entire countries.

Blockchain developers are devising alternatives, such as proof-of-stake or proof of authority, to address this issue. However, consensus protocols need to strongly resist falsification while remaining decentralized. It is a challenge to meet these strict criteria while maintaining adequate energy efficiency.

15.4. Addressing concerns around Quantum Computing

Advancements in quantum computing present a potential challenge. This is because quantum computers may be able to crack RSA and ECC encryption, widely used in blockchain protocols. If realized, an attacker could impersonate a party, alter transaction history or double-spend. While large, general-purpose quantum computers remain largely theoretical, it's a future threat that has stirred concern.

15.5. Societal Challenges

Blockchain's adoption across all sectors of society faces significant barriers. For individuals who lack technology literacy, the prospect of managing cryptographic keys or operating digital wallets is daunting. There are also serious concerns related to illicit activities such as money laundering or smuggling, facilitated by the pseudonymity typical in many blockchain implementations.

Addressing these challenges requires technical solutions, comprehensive regulation, and global cooperation. Education will play a central role in increasing awareness, demystifying the technology, and promoting its responsible use.

15.6. Response to Critics

Blockchain has been criticized as a solution looking for a problem. While it is innovative, critics argue it has been appropriated into areas that may not be a natural fit. Critics also point to alternatives that may solve problems more efficiently without fully resorting to decentralization.

However, from another perspective, blockchain is merely a tool in the toolset for problem-solving. It is not a solution in and of itself. With this mindset, organizations could derive benefits by utilizing blockchain in situations where it makes sense: to enhance transparency, remove intermediaries, reduce cost and time, increase trust and establish non-repudiable proof of transactions.

While blockchain faces constraints and critical voices, its potential benefits far outstretch these challenges. The technology is still evolving; complexities will be addressed, and efficiencies realized as greater understanding and application are achieved. It is not limited to cryptocurrencies but expands into a host of applications across numerous sectors. Its true potential may be yet to come. And as research continues, it will further inform the development and reduce the impact of the constraints and criticisms listed above.

The road to blockchain's widespread adoption is complicated by technical constraints, legislative gray areas, environmental concerns, and societal challenges. However, by understanding these issues and developing forward-thinking solutions, we could navigate this path more effectively, unlock blockchain's full potential, and solidify its position as a major disruptor in our era.

Chapter 16. Shaping Regulations: The Legal Landscape of Blockchain

As with all innovative technologies, the initial stages of wide-scale adoption also involve the adaptation of legal and regulatory schemes. Blockchain is no different. The technology has shown immense potential to transform various sectors, operating beyond borders, and indeed beyond conventional regulatory oversight. Its decentralized nature and unique features generate novel challenges for regulators worldwide, necessitating an in-depth understanding and innovative approach.

16.1. Regulatory Challenges of Blockchain Technology

Understanding blockchain technology and its possibilities is just the first step in accepting it. The next phase requires the construction of appropriate regulatory mechanisms that can adapt to the novel technical and operational complexities introduced by blockchain. Here are some key areas where this task may prove challenging:

1. **Decentralization:** In a conventional centralized environment, regulation ensures stability and accountability through a trusted central entity. However, blockchain's lack of a central authority confounds traditional law enforcement mechanisms. Legal and regulatory mechanisms must therefore evolve to address the challenges raised by decentralization.

2. **Cross-border Operations:** Blockchain operates globally, with nodes that can be located anywhere in the world. This makes it challenging to frame regulations within the existing territorial

jurisdictions. Regulators must tackle the intricate conflict and harmony of jurisdictional laws, especially concerning blockchain's applications like digital currencies.

3. **Privacy and Security:** Despite encrypted transactions and anonymity being a core feature, concerns regarding privacy and data protection exist in the blockchain space. More regulatory efforts are necessary to balance the benefits of transparency with the protection of user data.

4. **Illicit Activities:** Blockchain's pseudonymous nature has been misused for conducting illicit activities, such as money laundering and financial fraud. This demands regulatory mechanisms targeting these malicious uses.

16.2. Adapting Existing Legal Frameworks

While blockchain necessitates new regulatory strategies, existing legal frameworks in areas such as contract law, property law, and financial regulations may already provide some level of applicable oversight. It is vital, therefore, for lawmakers to incorporate blockchain into the existing legal fabric rather than wholly recrafting the laws.

1. **Contract Law:** Smart contracts generated on blockchain protocols could be legally binding if they meet all legal requirements of a contract such as offer, acceptance, consideration, and intention. Laws must be adapted to recognize these digital contract systems and the automatic enforcement they provide.

2. **Property Law:** The assignment of digital assets or cryptocurrencies to individuals or entities implies the need for adjustments in property law. Existing property laws should evolve to account for the unique way digital assets are owned,

transferred, and inherited.

3. **Financial Regulations:** Blockchain applications in the financial sector necessitate a revision of existing securities and banking laws. Regulatory bodies need to ensure that such developments adhere to enterprise risk management, consumer protection, and transparency standards.

16.3. Constructive Policy Approaches

The novelty and complexity of blockchain technology demand a proactive, yet balanced policy approach to foster innovation while mitigating risks. This involves promoting regulatory clarity and predictability, through methods such as regulatory sandboxes, or policy labs where new approaches can be safely tested.

Let's explore some of the policy approaches:

1. **Regulatory Sandboxes:** Regulatory sandboxes create a 'safe space' for businesses to test innovative products, services, and business models without fear of legal repercussions. These foster dialogue between innovators, regulators, and stakeholders, helping craft appropriate laws.

2. **International Cooperation:** As a global technology, the harmonization of blockchain regulations between countries can encourage its adoption and minimize legal uncertainties. International forums where policymakers can share experiences and align rules are therefore crucial.

3. **Public-Private Partnerships (PPPs):** Involving private stakeholders in decision-making processes can yield sophisticated regulatory designs. PPPs deliver a dual advantage: the private sector can influence lawmaking, and lawmakers can better understand the nuances of blockchain technology.

16.4. Leading Regulatory Practices Globally

Several countries have emerged as leaders in adopting blockchain-friendly regulations, each demonstrating unique strategies and lessons for others. Below are a few noteworthy examples:

1. **Estonia:** Estonia has pioneered e-governance, with several public services running on blockchain. Policies here provide explicit legal status for blockchain technology, enabling strong digital identity solutions and secure, efficient public services.

2. **Switzerland:** Switzerland's "crypto valley" serves as a global hub for blockchain startups. The Swiss government has established clear-cut guidelines for Initial Coin Offerings (ICOs) and created an accommodating environment for blockchain-based business models.

3. **Malta:** The "blockchain island" of Malta provides a comprehensive legal framework catering to different applications of blockchain. This includes three separate acts regulating digital innovation, virtual financial assets, and innovative technology arrangements and services.

4. **Singapore:** Monetary Authority of Singapore (MAS), the city-state's central bank, offers a regulatory sandbox for fintech innovations including blockchain. MAS has also issued guidelines on digital token offerings, elucidating regulatory considerations and compliance standards.

The growing understanding, acceptance, and application of blockchain technology across various sectors heighten the need for appropriate legal and regulatory measures. While it demands a rethinking and reformation of outdated frameworks, the resulting regulation should facilitate innovation, offer protection from illicit activities, and foster a productive blockchain ecosystem worldwide. In conclusion, the legislative and the regulatory mechanisms set today will undoubtedly shape the future of blockchain technology and its applications. Thus, it is imperative for these mechanisms to be comprehensive, flexible, and adaptive to ensure a healthy progression of this transformational technology.

Chapter 17. Preparing for the Future: Adapting Your Business for Blockchain

The pervasive rise of digital technologies is undermining many traditional business models, and propelling the world into an era of unprecedented innovation and disruption. One such novelty, blockchain technology, has the potential to revolutionize a wide array of sectors. It can decentralize operations, increase transparency, provide robust security, eliminate intermediaries, and more. As our world increasingly embraces this digital pivot, it becomes incumbent on businesses to understand and adapt to these technological transformations. This necessitates a strategic shift - a shift required not just to survive in this new age, but also to leverage the potential benefits of blockchain.

17.1. Understanding the Basics of Blockchain

Before we delve into the specifics of integrating blockchain into your business, we need to demystify the concept. Blockchain is a type of distributed ledger - an ever-growing database of transactions that is duplicated and stored across a network of computers (nodes). Each block within this chain carries a set of transactions, and are linked together using cryptographic principles.

Due to its architecture, blockchain ensures that all transactions are secure, transparent, and immutable, making it an ideal solution for any process that involves transfer of assets or recording of transactions. Its applications span various industries, from finance and healthcare to supply chain, legal, and more.

17.2. Recognizing the Blockchain Potential for Your Business

The first step towards adapting your business to blockchain technology is to identify the key areas where blockchain can offer the most impact. Various factors come into play here:

1. Data security: Does your business handle sensitive data that requires high security standards?

2. Transparency: Is there a need for enhanced transparency in your business operations, maybe in your supply chain or transactions?

3. Trust: Could your business benefit from a system that instills trust in users by its transparent and unalterable nature?

4. Efficiency: Could removing intermediaries in your processes, or automating them, lead to significant cost and time savings?

If your business needs align with at least one of these factors, chances are you could benefit from integrating blockchain technology.

17.3. Getting Started With Blockchain: Forming Your Strategy

Adapting to blockchain means reshaping your business' future. However, a clear strategy is paramount when implementing such transformative technology. Here are some essential steps to consider:

1. Define Your Objectives: Clearly articulate why you want to integrate blockchain into your business. The objectives should align with your business strategy and serve to improve some aspect of your operations.

2. Identify the Blockchain Type: Depending on your needs, you may

opt for a public, private, or consortium blockchain. Each of these has its unique features and pros and cons.

3. Seek Expertise: Blockchain is a complex technology that requires specialized skills. Consider recruiting or consulting with experts who have practical experience in blockchain implementation.

4. Design and Test a Prototype: Before a full rollout, develop a prototype to identify potential obstacles. This initial version can help you determine the value blockchain can bring to your business.

5. Plan for Integration: Map out how the new system will coexist or interact with your current systems. This includes data migration, user training, and support strategies.

6. Implementation and Iteration: Roll out the implementation in phases, allowing for adjustments and adaptations as you go. Keep track of performance metrics and adjust your strategy and goals as needed.

17.4. Ensuring Regulatory Compliance

Compliance with local and international regulations is paramount while integrating any new technology, and blockchain is no exception. Ensuring that your system abides by all the necessary data privacy, cybersecurity, anti-money laundering, and other pertinent regulations is essential. Regular audits and compliance checks should be an integral part of your blockchain strategy.

17.5. Leveraging Blockchain Benefits

Blockchain adoption doesn't just prepare your business for the future; it offers various immediate benefits. Enhanced transparency can foster trust with consumers, vendors, and stakeholders, while the high level of security reduces instances of fraud. Coupled with the efficiency of automation and the elimination of intermediaries, blockchain could offer tangible cost savings.

Blockchain technology is not a one-size-fits-all solution, but with the right strategy, it can be harnessed to drive significant improvements. The journey to integrating blockchain into your business can be as transformative as the technology itself, shaping stronger, more efficient, and more secure business models ready to thrive in the future. Embrace the blockchain revolution, and prepare to redesign the future of your business.